I0137218

BITTERROOT

by Abena Songbird

Freedom Voices
San Francisco, California
2000

Some of these poems/songs have appeared previously in :

Unsomo RedClay (1992, North Carolina)
Watch Out!, We're Talking (1994, Glide Word Press)
Cups, The Cafe Magazine (San Francisco, Vol. #3 Mar. 1995)
Street Spirit (San Francisco, Nov. 1996),
*Image And Imagination: Encounters with the Photography of
    Dorothea Lange* (San Francisco, 1997, Freedom Voices)
Moccasin Telegraph (WordCraft Circle of Native Writers &
    Storytellers. Vol. 3, #5&6, Aug.-Nov. 1997)
Fourteen Hills: The S.F.S.U. Review (Vol.4, #2 Spring/Summer
    1998)
Pacific Vision (Spring 1998)
National Library of Poetry (Nov. 1998)
They're Calling Us Home (1998, Cedar & Sage Music)
The Spirit in the Words - Moving People through Poetry (1999
    Daimler/Chrysler)
My Home as I Remember (2000 Natural Heritage/Natural
    Heritage, Toronto)

Copyright © 2000 Freedom Voices
All Rights Reserved
Edited by Ben Clarke and Kitty Costello
Produced at Red Star Black Rose in the U.S.A.
Cover and book design by Ben Clarke & Abena
Songbird Traditional Abenaki beaded bag by Nancy Naylor

P.O. Box 423115 San Francisco, CA 94142
www.freedomvoices.org
info@freedomvoices.org
ISBN: 978-0915117-06-2

For Lucy Pelkey Lafountain (1852-1927),
Marie LaFountain Truso (1873-1966),
Howard Bernard Naylor (1930-1970),
the Abenaki Paquettes/Pelkeys/Peltier "hide skinners"
family,
the songbirds,
and Mary TallMountain.

Acknowledgments

With much love and appreciation
"tout sweet" - all the tears and laughter
to the following people (and all others)
who listened and believed
helped me smooth out the rough spots
and flush out
a voice:

To Simon Ortiz, who started it all and showed me the
path; Janice Mirikitani,the poet of Glide Church, for the
years of teaching me how to write by reading, and lis-
tening to your poems/prose of dignity and justice; Rafiq
Bilal, for all the support and honing; Teveia Clarke,
Mary Jean Robertson, for you constant encouragement
and sharing of Mary TallMountain's writings and stories

With love for breath and the word:

Harvest McCampbell, Peter BrokenLeg, Sabrina Taylor,
Margot Pepper, Shar Suke, Ben Clarke, Kitty Costello,
Makita Groves, Rose Arrieta ,Nancy "Six Hawks" Naylor,
MorningStar Supnet, Wanda Sabir, Mary Jane "Dunks"
Naylor,

All the songbirds and "word warriors" still counting ver-
bal coup: Culture of Rage, Midnight Voices, Ulali,
Suhier Hammad, Without Rezervation, A.K. Black,
Imani, Wayquay, Asha Bandele, Aisha Bilal, Kamiko
Joy.

All the Indians everywhere for an unending supply of
humor, irony, tears and beauty

And those who hear the same drum:

Buffy St. Marie, John Trudell, Jim Pepper, Joy Harjo
Louise Erdrich, Adrian Louis, Rita Joe, Elizabeth Woody,
Thomas Swann, Joseph Bruchac, Jim Northrup, Susan
Power, Denise Sweet, Simon Ortiz, Velma Wallis, Cheryl
Savageau, Jack Forbes, Charles DeLint, Sherman Alexie,
Linda Hogan, M. Scott Momaday, Louis Owens, Mary
TallMountain , Anne Dunne, Vickie Sears, and on...

Contents

Introduction

When I first encountered Abena Songbird's poetry about ten years ago I was immediately entranced with it. Abena and I are from the same part of Indian country; she from Vermont, me from Connecticut where the three rivers meet.

When I was four years old a poacher trapped a red fox in a steel trap. The mother gnawed the paw off her kit, trying to free it. My father helped me raise that fox, we gave it a balsalm foot. When it grew old enough, we took it thirty miles from our home and released it in the woods. In one week it came back. Then we took it sixty miles. It took one month to come back. Abena's poetry is like this. Even though she travels widely and may be miles away from her physical origins her poetry keeps coming home.

A Supervisor on the San Francisco Board many years ago, was speaking at the Indian center and declared "many Indians live in cars". I don't think she understood that we found cars an improvement over some of the housing we were being offered at the time. If this Supervisor had read Abena's poem *Stretching the Dough* perhaps she'd have clue.

Abena's poetry displays a rare understanding of both Native people from the country and from urban settings—the street. I'm very touched always by Abena's poetry and I'm so glad she's published! Now it will be easier to share her words and meanings with friends and family. Reading these poems sometimes I just weep. Sometimes I dance and am delighted. What more can you ask of a poet than that?

Once in the yuwipi ceremony I came to this wonderful clear meadow, removed from all the stress and anxiety of living today. And this is a place that Abena can take me to in her poetry. She is indeed a poet in her very thinking.

She has captured bubbles of worlds that are vastly different and strung them together making the beading of her work very rich, very colorful, very sensitive.

Bitterroot is a special medicine.

Teveia Clarke
WebWorks Indigenous People's Archive
San Francisco, July 2000

Beginning

why did I feel the need to write
birthing sounds
to grasp wildly for
a grounding stone
when the wind blew through
these bones
in dreams
I died
more than once
eaten by mangy dogs
torn to bits
shot in the head
and the heart
met the transition angel
more than once
she was beautiful
all black and purple
"you should never touch
the wound that kills you"
she told me on her way
leading me down the hall
to my new job assignment
I tired soon
of being a ghost
but not before
I played a few
jokes on the living
invisible I etched Boo!
on frosty windowpanes
in front of startled
unsuspecting faces
before my impatient angel
smirking pushed me forward
to join the other recently unemployed
I died more than once
fell from a great distance

yet lived to tell it
and it seemed most
urgent
the telling
to get it right
to connect with
someone else
who
died
to
live

Beer Soaked Chants

Stretching the Dough

this Indian lives on the corner of Haight and Masonic, literally. He greets me as sister Red Road. He always apologizes, especially after the dirty jokes. He nickel and dimes people but he has turkey medicine. His mother every few months scrapes together a Western Union check that she sends him to go home to the pueblo, sober up and pick piñons and chilies. He takes $30.00 and buys avocados, lemons, chips and canned salsa, spreads them gingerly on the sidewalk to share with the other Indians and the homeless tribe. "Will they let me serve them? Will they eat my offering?" he worries as he knows his hands are dirty but they keep the bathrooms in the park locked at night and he can't keep clean...

this Indian runs up to me in the city because I'm another Indian - to say "Hey, what's up!" He explains the spreading stain on his jeans: "It's just beer, not pee!" An important distinction - we are a proud people. My house gets robbed on Tuesday *this Indian* tells me what to do: " You get fishing line and some 3 prong fishhooks, like for salmon or northern pike and string them all along the inside of your car or windows. When they reach their hand through the glass the barb gets them good and if they try to pull it out it just embeds further and then you've got your ID." He knows this guy who was landed real good, still ripping and thrashing at the hook as it impaled a major artery in his arm.

this Indian who owned the car came up and even offered to drive the bloody thief to the hospital...

this Indian is traditional, he makes his living on the drum playing from Powwow to Powwow. He asks me how to deal with the IRS I tell him I called them once. I told them that according to my tribal Treaties of 1713, 1717, the Jay Treaty of 1794, the Washington Treaties of 1812, 1842, the Ghant Treaty of 1815 and the self-determination Act of 1968, I didn't have to pay taxes...he put me on hold for 45 minutes. He came back on the line laughing and said, "You're right. You don't have to pay taxes on anything you hunt, fish or trap within the boundaries of Odanak and running southerly, parallel to Trois Rivieres, etc."

this Indian says, "Well maybe I'll do that then..." thanks - courtesy of Indian Reparations Service (IRS).

this Indian friend had her grandmother transit this year. She has dreams of her walking down the road by her old home with two hawk feathers in her flowing silver hair. In the sweat she feels a gentle wind blow across her face.

this Indian also had her grandmother pass over this year. She has dreams of her Unci: She comes hollering her name and saying, "I haven't seen you in awhile. Get over here and give me a perm, you can't get them over here."

this Indian lives at the Civic Center corner. He's a giant, over 6'9" and a moviestar. When he's sober he shyly edges toward the drum at gatherings and sings songs in his own language...
this Indian was adopted out, split up from his eleven brothers, sisters and cousins and placed in foster homes. This year he wouldn't enter the roundhouse. He's not ready, he walks with his anger. When the Pomo elder showed us how to spiral 3 times to enter, he walked away. He has too much respect for tradition to lie.

this Indian is 10 years old!

this Indian sits on the sidewalk an loosens the concrete with a spoon. They say her mind is gone but she has an agenda. When enough sidewalk is loosened people trip and fall. She grins, "Now maybe they'll stop and respect the Mother!"

these Indians in the city celebrate the earthquakes, thunders, blackouts, rain, windstorms, lightning - it's the cleansing- the time when other people start to act like Indians...

these Indians help each other laugh, no matter how hard life can be, and share and share and share whatever they got - gossip, a dirty joke, a story, a bottle, cigarettes, coffee or a song...

and sometimes you'll see this young woman, she may be Tohono O'odham, with a hint of a smile on her face, smudges of white flour dust her dance shawl.

They say she and her mother stretched that fry bread and fed 300 Indians on the Oakland streets the other day...

Some saw the Creator in that dough...

I was raised on a song there
I done right, I done wrong there
and it's true I belong there
and it's true it's my home
going back to the woodlands
going back to the snow
going back to the hills
and the valley below
I'll return like a poor man
or a king if God wills
but I'm on my way home
to my piney wood hills

—Buffy St. Marie
Piney Wood Hills

Bitterroot

a plug my sister sent me
I keep in my sweetgrass basket
for when I get sore throats
when it closes up and threatens to
take me back to the silent time
the time I didn't
talk
bitter plant
"take your bitters with the sweet" - a sure sign of
maturity my friend Harvest reminds me
her Oswego grandmother said the medicine you
need to cure you
is right there where you fall
I fell at the ocean's edge
three thousand miles from Vermont
the starting place - Ndakinna
but even city sidewalks got
dandelion, licorice, muskmallow, mullein
pushing up undaunted
dry, powdered with car exhaust
through cracks of concrete
their damp leaves to squelch

some wounds
that
seem too big to heal

I fell into circles
talking circles of recovery
years I spent in 12 steps
twice, three times a week
reliving a family history
of alcoholism, codependency
rage, shame and fear
my dreams
peppered with night sweats
shaking memories
yet
slowly uncovering a healing
pushing up as through concrete
like stubborn weeds
a root
deep threads of remembrance
that I am Indian
that I have a history, traditions
years I have 12-stepped
until I learned a two step
around the drum, circling
sweats that cleansed my spirit
bitterroot
a way to heal
soothing my throat
of the silence that's shadowed me
since childhood
in school when they called me "smiley"
because I would not talk
I smiled
a peace offering to
get them off my back
smiled so
they wouldn't kick my ass
now the silence comforts me
a way of walking on this earth
a way of listening

and when I dreamed of dad
he'd be behind glass
pounding his drum
so small and unthreatening

the bow and arrows were
on the ground
I picked them up
now
he wouldn't hurt me
now
his spirit
is guiding me
still
a bitterroot

The Alcoholic Church

Oh holy spirit
of the alcoholic church
daddy pickled on spirits
hunting his Abenaki shadow

My sister says he thinned my hair
when I was ten
said I looked "too wild"...

Oh holy spirit of the alcoholic
church
daddy pickled in spirits
stalking his shadow

he'd stalk the deer in November
eating beef jerky
sipping whiskey in
the stillness
the spirits came down then...
the spirits came down
he just wanted to rest
curled like a fawn
in high grass
later
a cirrhotic hemorrhage
steaming like deer blood
in the crisp
November woods
a savage red
his last warpaint

his scalped spirit
finally free
little deer spirit
darts through the thicket

Bruised Fruit

for Jan, who taught me about justice, dignity and the word

A prostitute came into the corner market
She brushed my should at the fruit stand
She asked me which pears were the ripest
I said the ones most bruised

> I work in a church with bruised people
> people who have been molested
> people who have been forced into intern-
ment camps

> people who have lived with drunks
> people who have known madness
> people who have been through divorce
> people who have been ravaged by drug
and alcohol addiction

these are the juiciest, the ripest, most alive peo-
ple I know

> I had a dream that a deer high on a hill
had its hoof splayed
> In a wire trap and you, Jan, helped me
free the deer

> Somewhere in that dream mirrors my
days here at Glide
> Where my bruised, trapped self longs to
flow freely
> like the words across this page
> or in a song
> like that deer leaping
> freely
> across that meadow in the sun

Scattered Maple Leaves

Big sister my
nanny goat
little brother bobcat
didn't we survive 30°
degrees below and fallin'
snowdrift giants and
blackice
the sting of frostbite
raspberry briars
and burdock burrs
weren't we
lonely dirtroad runaways
maple leaf rag
midnight starwalkers
daddy's gone again

didn't we survive
late night ruckus
feral dogs
attacking our sheep
daddy's home again
with bottles smashing
a nightly thunder
divorce, divorce, divorce
dinner table preaching
beer soaked chanting
"if I should die tomorrow"...
didn't we witness our history
in woodstove cracklin'
Winter kitchens
with rats in our barn
rats in our pantry
rats in our kitchen

daddy's just wrestling
don't you cry
roughhousing
with
loneliness
fending poverty

from our door
shut off in separate rooms
dark and looming
years of never speaking
scattered maple leaves
passed off to strangers
when mom's working
awkward and ugly rites of passage
with poor, urine-perfumed backwoods
trailer girls
and tough, townie white boys
smoking and swearing
plucking and shucking
pet chickens
their scrawny necks
sacrificed
on tree stumps
those chickens

but weren't we sugar on snow
butternuts and rootbeer
venison and frogslegs
green beans
sweet corn
fishing and camping
always fishing and camping
climbing some mountain
daddy
staring off
to future untrod trails
star walker

sister my sister
nanny goat
brother bobcat
my
didn't we survive
like scattered maple leaves
thrown
from
the tree

Pressure Creates Diamonds

Dawn

His face could take a piercing
knife or a needle
with no expression
anesthetized/Lt. Calley's finger over flame
a forced bravado
steely
ice cold

He was driving fueled with bennies
when he churned up the dust
on that dry, dirt road
she had long been standing on

Barely out of high school
fresh from a darkened theater
"The Deer Hunter"
was still rolling in her
mind's celluloid
her thoughts
a focused arrow
fresh from the quiver
equating pain and suffering
with love, romance
her father, the deer hunter
dead six years
she was still looking
for his traces
tracking a ghost
through white man's movies
and books
then
with her thumb to the wind
on the back roads, woods, bars
and men
of this country

He was driving with a trunk full of smuggled

diamonds
from Indochina; the 'Nam Vet's employment
security
they robbed the Buddhist temples
tucked in the mountains of Viet Nam
of gold and diamonds and
sold them to the brokers on Manhattansí
         diamond row

Noon

He taught her his survival skills
the hunter and the hunted
how to reveal nothing
stare down the enemy
he illustrated
by pouring hot coffee
on her sandaled foot
he bought her tomato juice
said, "You need iron when you're running in the
jungle"

when he pulled into a K-Mart to buy her clothes
something snapped in her
he said she must look less haggard
as he pulled into a truckstop hotel
he told her of the time he proposed
to his wife
how he hid the ring in this rainbow trout
she was cleaning
she almost sliced her finger
off in her surprise
at the diamond that spilled from
that gutted trout

he began brushing her hair
in long strokes
that hypnotized
her own reflection in the mirror
at 19 she was wild

fresh on the surface/coltish
with hair in long streams
reaching below her ass
she was stalling...

he led her back toward
the bed
and stroked her
she felt nothing but numbness
touched herself fast to come
to relax, sleep, escape
he was touched
thought she was shy
like the women in Saigon
he had forced himself on
as he pumped on her
he bragged proudly of horrors
rape and murder
as if it had honor
those women of Vietnam
couldn't afford the price either

The pumping seemed like hours
he was still limp, the bennies
she began to feel like that wet trout
cold, clammy and gutted
but no diamonds
spilled from her mouth

she rolled over and feigned sleep
it had to be right...
her breathing had to be smooth, not too shallow
she knew somehow he'd kill her
if he knew she couldn't come
if he suspected she feared him
if he knew she saw his fear
that he was a "jacked-up psycho"
worse than Christopher Walken's roulette mad-
ness
his impotency was ready to crush her
like those Saigon statistics

she thanked Spirit for bennies and "ladies of the
night"
as his attention was caught by all movement
and sound
a true predator
he spent the night flicking the blinds open and
shut
watching the girls come and go
from the trucker's rooms

Morning

Booty
He was hunched over unrolled black velvet
his monocle poised over diamonds
eyes red from sleeplessness
he showed her his "ladies"
and rolled two of the smallest diamonds
in a plastic bag
jammed them into a matchbook cover
he told her: "This is how you hide them when
you get to DC. Take them to a jewelers. Tell
them they are from your grandmother's brooch
or something. This will take care of you.
They're worth at least $450.00 each. They are
uncut."

Such fatherly advice...
when she got to DC hungry and homeless
she spent nights in bus stations and a shelter
for the insane.
she snuck into a fifth- floor dorm at Washington
University
to get burned out in a major fire
stumbled around this nation's capitol
smelling of smoke
and watched the homeless warm themselves on
the steam that
rose in the winter air from sewer grates
she saw the ghetto two hundred feet from the

presidential lawn
thumbing that matchbook like a fetish
finally she took it to a jewelers.

They didn't believe her
they seemed suspicious
they said the diamonds were too small
too rough, uncut
she was afraid
Capitol Hill, The Deer Hunter, that hotel
those smugglers, the ghettos, the homeless, the
lies of whitemen...
her father's not here

she fell from that store
and ran to a restaurant
where she flushed their brilliance down a toilet.

Pressure creates diamonds

Raking the Roots

The Roots, the Bark, the Sap of the Heart*

a snap of branch and twig
a crunch of
frost-laden leaf
announces
my winter walk
I pull and tug
the root
that surfaces
at the foot
of the spruce

searching a people
a passage
from Odanak
gliding down the
St. Lawrence
last name
ties to a people
unsmiling photos of
dark women
Victorian buns
of coiled braids lay
like snakes, long sleeping
on their heads
loose breathings of soft
supple skins
of fringe traded
for corsets of calico in
flower prints
a piece of dried
tobacco
sweetgrass woven around
a basket
a braid wrapped
in smoked skins
grieving a dead relative

my snowshoes scout
in spiral direction
mimicking grouse's
warning
from her nest

I pull and
rake the roots
that snap
and curl in my hands
dried
umbilical chords
stiff reins pulling
in all my relations—Lôgodamwôgan
lacing the birch basket
that holds a great-great grandmother
traveling up from
near permafrost
up from dead leaf mulch
twisting
around bones of deer
fallen to harsh winter's
hunger
spilling
acorn caches of red and gray
squirrel
through groves of pine
aspen and birch
around mushroom
rings of faerie
past rabbit's hutch
and fox burrows

I rake
and pull
from
cities
far removed

(After a short story by Thomas Swann.)

My Mother Is a Painter
for mamere "dunk"s

My mother is a painter
she painted three
masterpieces
with
sparrow's hair
tufts of nutty brown
noses that are broad
strong and peaked
chins that dimple
and
jut

my mother is a painter
she painted three canvases
with
eyes of hazel
fawn and sable
bodies sloped
and
rounded
curved and snaked
like rivers
with
mountainous
hollows and rolls

my mother is a painter
from her womb
she squeezed
an
ocean of color
a splatter and bleed
of ochre
cinnamon and teal
chaparral, brick
and terra cotta
azure, coral and
burnt sienna

sturdy trees
that whistle in
the wind
canoes
deft and watertight
flutes with reeds of willow
that bend
but do not break
my mother is a painter
who paints
her mother
with
elder down of snowgoose hair
words
of wit and vinegar
laughter
sweet
as maple sap
my mother is a painter
who paints
Mother Earth's gift of every day
hummingbird feeds
from her tubers
summer's shadow
stretches
across her
lawn

My mother is a painter...
now she paints her
greatest work
she dips her brush in
her spring
of
dreams
and paints thoughts of
new beginnings
never ending in a circle
of sixty seven
stones

The Grammy Awards

I am watching the annual
Grammy Awards
that night I had a dream:

there is a mesquite tree
two crows are perched
in a craggy limb
singing a chorus:

"Stay in tune..."
"Stay in..."
"Stay tuned".
Out of the woods comes an elder
with snowy owl hair
in her hands
she carries a bowl
a basket
her eyes sparkle
in the moonlight
lighting little fires
that illuminate my soul
she is laughing and handing me
the sweetgrass basket
and
I laugh
The Grammy Awards

Mamere Truso

The Grammy Awards

Furry, sticky butternuts smashed
with a hammer
on old newspaper
their nutty meal popped
quickly
into hungry mouths

spruce gum
scraped fresh from the tree
pitch molded
by aching jaws
on the way to the winter spring

milkweed pillows
stuffed with fine silk
fingers sticky
dripping with thick, white milk
carted in a wagon
sold door to door

first strawberries and sweet corn
picked with the
songs of thanks
braids wrapped and
coiled tightly on her head
like a shiny
black garter snake

calico cotton dresses
and quilts
flour sacks pieced
patiently and sewed
into stars and cabins
round wire-rimmed glasses
perched intently
on her nose
hops pulled up
by the root

boiled slowly
steeped for a spell
to let it breath
then wrapped around
her daughter's stomach
to relieve a cramping belly

potatoes
wrapped in an old stocking
on a grandbaby's head
draw the poisons
while feeding him
willow bark for a blinding headache
a corncob pipe lit up
after every meal
filled with the herb mixture that
settles her stomach
clears her mind
for prayer
red willow, comfrey, sage
her daily reverie with
the Creator

Natty Johnny Banks
Silver City , New Mexico
Christmas Eve 1979

evening sun on
pink adobe
church bells mixed with the
laughter of brown-skinned boys and girls
and all those luminarias
greasy brown paper bags with sand and candles
lighting up the night
such beauty
so simple
reminders that I'm far from mountain country
snow
but there was Johnny
deep into a Richie Rich comic
Johnny was a
natty dresser
red cravat tied just so
looking like a singing cowboy
with his lizard skin cowboy boots
and his tight-fitting western shirts
bright orange or mint green
embroidered with colored bric-a-brac and rain-
bow ribbon
topped by a crushed black felt beaver hat

He liked to pose by the new Cadillacs
just like Ritchie Rich
we had a date on Christmas Eve to see Snow
White
and the Seven Dwarfs
this theme of white
stark
against a contrast of desert
yuccas and Mexican graveyards
the graves mounded up with stones and bright
plastic flowers
and Johnny all purple black

I wondered did Johnny identify with the dwarfs?
even Richie Rich was a white boy kid
like Billy the Kid in a Silver City jail cell
baby-faced outlaw who couldn't fit in
chip-toothed and simple

This black cowboy and one Indian
misfits
roaming those streets
Johnny was long
 6' 5", probably 45 years old
mentally about 8 or 9
he loved Disney
my partner in crime and fun

Christmas Eve dinner was
Hormel chili in a vacuum sealed can
I broke the aluminum lid in my haste
to get at those petrified chunks
in that Laundromat -
Mexican kids, little vatos terrorizing me
with their new motorized scooter
tearing up and down the aisles
lonely
no Johnny
those kids and I
pooled our change to get vending machine
Christmas candy
hoped he was okay
wondered did he live on the street
his clothes were always pressed so
clean stiffly starched
so someone was looking
out for him
maybe he, like Ritchie
had a "Gloria*"

*Ritchie's comic strip girlfriend

Oh Drum!

Oh drum!
bones on bodhran
wildly beating
variegated fires
in heart chambers
dancing
feet stomping
growing louder
now softer
in swells
waves cresting
drumming
journeys
past potato fields
long fallow
to evergreen
gently swaying
summoning mists across the heather

Oh drum!
northern drum, traditional
swelling
song
through thick hoarfrost
hair-raising tremors
lifting
over groves of birch and pine
a flutter of wings
the heart flies
dreaming

Albuquerque

Rosa, Lorraine and me
two Indians and a Mexican
hunched over dim lit cubicles
2'x3'
the stinging scent of acetone wafting
a sharp cloying cloud
singeing nosehairs
not sweet like grandmother's lilacs

That summer
our elbow fused
we worked in booths separated only by
thin partitions and radios blaring
KUNM University of New Mexico
mariachi, zydeco, chicken scratch and powwow
drums
competing with the roar of the sanders
we worked

Albuquerque

our hands poised with picks
we prodded and maneuvered
the slightest slivers of turquoise
brilliant flecks of sky
so optimistic
forced into jigsaw shapes of butterfly, thunder-
birds, buffalo, snakes
pink conch, abalone, turquoise and coral red
stones of connection
sky and sea
elbow to elbow
we arranged new forms
the sun in cement
in a low-ceilinged
dimly- lit concrete warehouse
we worked
separated only by
the thinnest of cotton masks
that trapped and pushed those fumes

further up one's nose

Rose - Chicana mother of twins
drove her award-winning low ride
a mint green vintage thunderbird
lectured me on a history
her family's inheritance - acequias
water rights, major domos
and her teenage twin's psychic abilities
as we clustered around the long metal
lunch table separated in groups
only by our foods
Cambodian, Laotian - rice and fish
we coveted Rosa's tamales
much preferred to the aluminum lunch truck
parked daily in the outdoor parking lot
with it's stale food and jacked up prices
Lorraine passed the calabacitas, venison
green chili stew and fry bread and made
fun of the trinkets we inlaid with stories
of her family artisans who sold at Santa Fe
Indian market and the Albuquerque Fairgrounds
imagine women raised under a turquoise sky
in ancient pueblos of her people for over
ten thousand years
land where they continue ceremony
dancing , singing, drumming
their chests and fingers covered in gleaming sil-
ver
inlaid with the sky
protections - sacred healing stones
now hunched 8-10 hours a day in dimly lit
cement warehouses
perfumed with chemicals versus sage and cedar
to feed her children and grandchildren
on $7.00 an hour
no union here...
we all applied for this job one day by walking up
three
flights of stairs to a small cubicle

where a white man sat behind tinted glass
he could look down and see all of us on the
main floor
without being seen, while he made decisions
from his
desk on high
who should be promoted, who should be fired
we'd never see him

focused, bent over
heads pounding from the glues and resins
we worked long hours
hunched stiffly over minutia
those flecks of turquoise
frozen in acetate
baked, buffed and sanded
then polished to a high gloss
for cigarette lighters, belt buckles
money clips for tourists
occasionally Lorraine would sneak
something fancy into her designs to gift a grand-
daughter
who would be dancing at the Pueblo that year
while Rosa caught me up on *The Young and
Restless*
Victor Neuman's next move
and her daughter's latest predictions

throats hoarse we'd yell over
the steady echoes of the
large burners, ovens and fans
some days Lorraine's cries overpowered these
fans
as she was told of yet another relative
becoming roadkill on the highway by the Pueblo
or a statistic in a knife fight
a burner burst one day
the fires flared yellow-red
like the zuni sun
reflected in Rosa's widened eyes

flashbacks of the war chased the
the Cambodian/Laotian women screaming
to the only exit door
they clawed at it
as fire licked our heels

we then all became kin in our unemployment
I miss those women
I miss their elbows
I miss their laughter and stories
I see them in the turquoise sky

One Wail Rising

Cradled in Corn

My shadow is long
taller than these seeded cornstalks
tall enough to swallow
the sun
this was our playing place
my sisters/
squash and beans
we sang and circled
weaving and swaying
hands raised to the sun
now they lie beneath me
still and silent
my shadow is long
cradled in corn
rocking...
wrapped and shrouded
in this obsidian shaded shawl
of ancestors
grandparents holding me
cradled in corn
rock-a-bye baby
in the treetops
screaming crows dive
violently circle me
as I stand swaying
cradled in corn
my voice is theirs
comes in whispers
one wail rising
wind through dried corn stalks
their bones
rattling   rusted leaves
dance around me
mixed with dried cornsilk

the hair of the mother
the crows are screaming:
"this earth is puckered and parched
painted with their blood"
there are no tears left

cradled in corn
we planted the seeds
with songs
we made our dolls of
husk and cornsilk
we wrapped our tamales
in it's thick coat
our food
our play
our harvest
cradled in corn

my shadow is long
tall enough to swallow the sun
my silent dance partner
we are swaying
rocking
no tears left
I'm waiting for a new
flower
like the sun
to burst forth   in flame
then I'll sing
the Green Corn Song

We Have Names

We have names for places
places of flint
places of pine
Missisquoi
Cowasuk, Sokoki
names for river places
Winooski - onion river
Nebizonôbok - medicine springs
places of Tabaldak
chiseled by the Creator
places of spirit
names for the sacredness
of the land
Ndakinna - our land
Wabanaki - of the dawn
Alnôbak - the people

We Use Our Hands

Oceans and rivers
great lakes and streams
we are the dreamers
weaving the dreams

Oceans and rivers
great flow and ebb
we are the weavers
weaving the web...

When the Dawnland people ate songbirds
they set out their snares
shaped
like tiny snowshoes
wrapped with sinew
and hooked with the thinnest
horsehair nooses
a bird's leg would catch
the black hair pulled taut
ten and twenty birds
gave their songs to the people

when the Dawnland people
wove baskets
standing knee-deep in pulp
and ash shavings
lacings of spruce root
and incense of sweetgrass
art took on a new meaning
how many baskets
does it take
to feed a family
half a dozen in trade
for a week's worth of flour, molasses, tea
and cloth
from the settler's store

when my people made baskets
for over two hundred years to survive
you never saw their collection

proudly displayed
in their longhouses, wigwams, homes
they sat on white ladies mantles
filled with threads of silk and lace
or later with the cheap indigo
from the storekeeper's stock
their lips swollen from
flattening the porcupine quills
for the fancy quill
and splint boxes
they worked so hard
with antler-handled knives
draw shaves and axes
for so little...
pennies were pitched for
baskets
woven water tight
with our songs, dreams and stories
that held lives
that healed
with their sweetgrass scent

to sell meant to move
to uproot
downriver in birchbark canoe
later sled, train and steamship
setting up camp
stripping the sprucepoles
and forming the circle
shawling them in birchbark
laced tight, like our baskets
with the spruce root
or later with cloth tarpaper
that wouldn't
keep out the rain
traveling and selling to coastal summer resorts
in Canada, in Boston Commons and all over
N'dakinna (our land)
New England...
picking fiddleheads, potatoes, blueberries

claming and cleaning
in the white people's houses

The Dawnland people
lived a life by hands
and today get "museum" prices
for the baskets
they are "valued"
but sometimes they sit in dusty swap meets
and at antique dealers' stores
that only collectors can afford

acid rain is killing
the trees
they are dying from
the tops
down
and the pesticides on the grasses, roots
and sedge
burn sores on grandmother's lips
from Odanak
to the California Coast...

Oceans and rivers
great lakes and streams
we are the dreamers
weaving the dreams

Oceans and rivers
great flow and ebb
we are the weavers
weaving the web

Nana and the Mountain

The Grammy Awards

a hot July
leads her to the window
as she raises it a cool breeze
slips suddenly through
it rustles and whips
the curtains
coming closer she brushes
a cobweb away
from her face
it draws her eye outside
for a moment
"Noone was ever hurt
by a little Irish lace", she hears her mother say

she is startled by the mountain
Camel's Hump rises tall
looming in her view
now she hears a faint, thin sound in the breeze

almost like a whisper
it rises and grows
like the strain of a fiddle
now she hears it's song:

Lena
Leaping Lena
throw on your shawl of evergreen
your cloak of spruce and pine
Hazel is calling you
she sits in the saddle of Dawakbedenewadso
on the Hump of the Camel
at the nape of Crouching Lion
she is holding a deck
of cards
she wants you to join her

Leap, Lena
leap
she remembers walking

this mountain
in the spring
past tender curls of fiddleheads
past stinkin' benjamins
thrilled at the occasional jack-in-the-pulpit
and first strawberry blossoms

she is pulled by that clean, pure air
coming through her window
making her dizzy
with its incense
of cedar and tall pine
the cool reminds her of the Canadian peppermints
her mother always liked to suck
wintergreen
pink and white, round as pennies
it cleanses and renews her spirit
again she hears the funny music
coming from above:

Lena
put on your shawl of evergreen
your cloak of sweetest maple
Leap Lena
leap over mountains

Papa Lewis Jay
is waiting
all the Garveys were tree people
who knew the power
of a grove
Grandfather Charles has rosined
up his fiddle
he and Genny are sawing out a tune for you
they are calling you
to a junket on the mountain
to dance with those pretty legs of yours
they are sitting in the saddle
they are sitting on the hump
ready
for the journey home

Wild Geese

Your oiled oboe
linseed sheen on ebony
an African branch that
glistens and squeaks

Say:
Wild geese calling
wild geese squall

something sweet and earnest
as blowing trumpets from a blade
of summer grass

its song brings rivers
rivulets
beckoned by two moistened reeds

Say:
Wild geese come singing
wild geese call

When my soul seems frozen
in need of some
innocence
warmed by a clump of peony
teetering forward
from a sea of parted grasses
in the plump hand
of a child

I hear the Winter geese
honking
my heart melts like
ice on a spring lake

Say:
Wild geese soaring
wild geese squall

In the Bramble

wrestling in
the bramble
the prick of thorny
vines
inspire me to find
a clearing
in which I can catch
their juice
scenting your lips
a softest berry
when I
kiss them it's like
I catch blackberries
their plump and downy fur
crushed all over
your caramel skin
and suck
and lick their sweet
around the ring of your nipple
until it's stiff
like the bark of an oak

we smell a misty
vapor
as the sun bakes
those purple-black ripples
down our thighs
and I grab your hair
textured and thick
ropes of finest hemp
twisted sculpture
in my hands

so sweet and wild
the slight
sting of thorns
and the honey in
those berries

as we wrestle

we   make juice
honey, we make juice

Knocking Off the Horns

Leaders of America
your "Founding Fathers" patterned
directly from the Six Nations Iroquois
Confederacy in building
this country's constitution.
now
the Clan Mothers step forward
exercise their prerogative
"knock off your horns"

strip you of your titles
take back their reins of council fires
to burn away this mess
you sever your umbilical cord to the earth

the Clan Mothers Speak:
You are not fit to rule!

As the Wheel Turns

Thundereggs & Garnets
especially for Michael—I miss you,
Nancy, Peter, Heath, Dana & Lorraine, Teveia
and all us "recovery" Indians

to you drunk
three-sheets-to-the-wind
or behind the wheel
with some white thick fog
of a joint enclosing you

that day
your hand fit so perfectly
in the ancient petroglyph print
of your coyote people

the wheel turned and everything shifted

an avalanche of stone beings
layers of rock once dormant
groaning
grinding awake
up from rich sediment
raining thundereggs

did you forget
the unblinking
eyes of your grandparents watching
as deer
when you visited their graves

that day
your hand traveled
lengths of rigid spinal column
the sturgeon
was summoned
up from the bottomless lake
welcoming you home
ancient spirit

the wheel turned and everything shifted

waters spoke to you
rocks spoke to you
and Chief Joseph may smile
up at you
from the bottom
of your bottle

out of your hand full
of rock
natural garnet may spill
if you're lighting up
that crack pipe
the smoke may just swirl
touching you with fingers
of all those women and children
hiding on the Snake River
to rake you
with the claws
of BearPaw Mountain
grasping your spirit
clutching you
taking you in
reminding you of the
other pipe
the original way

My Broken Steed

this land
unlike a map
is not stagnant   unmoving
not fixed flat on a page
a frozen terrain
new rivers may be
carved daily
by logs fallen to lightening
deep channels
from the scat of deer, moose and bear
may grow the rarest blooms
tendril furls of green fern...

Intensive Care
Ramadan
1997

stroke (strok) n. blow; sudden seizure of illness,
misfortune

His head, too heavy for his shoulders
languid
sinking droops
bobbing slightly
thin streams of drool unhindered flow and catch
in pools
on his cotton-sheathed skin
this man, never at a loss for words, corrects the
Arabic of well-meaning
friends
praying over his death mask in intensive care
this man, keynote speaker/lecturer,
author, owner of the innovative, non-alcohol,
non-tobacco, culturally diverse
Bay Area nightclub, crack cocaine counselor,
community educator,
leader
my lover now for years
his words now mutterings
unstrung salad of words

eyes unfocused babbling jagged quatrains
uranian bolts
word streams hot-wired to his tongue
tumble in steady dirge
loud and driven
for me to catch in my sleepless vigil
I must pay attention and record his minutia
his leaps and bounds
"Abenaki - get this down!...where are you...you
weren't there..."
as if his sack of skin tries out first sound
in love with the vibrations
the sensation and not the structure of meaning
a new language
his word salad
disjointed and unattached
I strain to catch the intent behind the jumble
of cosmic detail, astrological configurations,
nightly news, names, dates,
random facts
Does he know where he is? Does he know what's
happened to him?
fluids stream from him
afterbirth for me to catch
in sterile plastic containers
like a new mother I sometimes
nod and guiltily miss his growth

my lover, my man, my fledgling
my broken steed
I laden his bed with talismans
river stones, buffalo and pyramids
a dreamcatcher, prayer beads, his walking stick
of crooked manzanita
sage, sweetgrass I send up when the nurses aren't
looking, frankincense oil,
Koran
prayer feathers
draw on all the prayers we have
Allah-hu-Akbar, Al-hamdulillah...Ramadan

I find they have an Indian doctor at Highland!
he tells the nurses not to touch the prayer feath-
ers
I pull this Pine Ridge Lakota doctor in for prayer
Tunkasila Oniwan
Mitakuye Oyasin
Allah-hu-Akbar, Al-hamdulillah...Ramadan

stroke (strok) n. to caress; to soothe, to pass
hand gently over

I bring food
concentrated juices
thick pureed roots   green gruel
ginger, echinachea, beet greens
herbal tinctures packed to infuse an instant cure
an energy boost
his dysphagic throat can't swallow
he's choking on life
his spit, itself too rich
if I was mama eagle I could ingest and regurgi-
tate his food myself
into his mouth
he must absorb food
he will be too thin - a stick
his left arm a shriveled wing - unmoving
paralyzed already emaciated
it's fingers curl, stiff talons
I stroke and stroke, rub like prayer beads
his hair thick matted dreads
have to be cut   they rot and disintegrate
in his daughter and my hands
like lichen wisps cleared from a rock
no blood runs down his entire left side
the runt of the nest
mama eagle licks this fur most
to stimulate early flight
days of bedside holding, talking and singing
friends emerge in stready droves
I save the crying for when he's asleep

and late night bus rides home from the hospital

when all the world
was a bucking horse
tree roots my tangled reigns

I lay flat on Mother Earth
felt the blood flow
in her trenched veins

when all the world
was a bucking horse
and you
my broken steed

I wept into earth's
tiny brook
and saw all my knots
had freed

when all the world
was a bucking horse
and witnessed
my nightly shaken cry

I prayed loudly in her face
the moon
and found new strength
this horse
won't die...

Two weeks

His eyes unglazed now clear
impossibly large
like a Madagascar lemur
a fledgling
his head, now upright
a steady trunk
but his legs wobble
his left leg
scrawny still not working
they give him wheels
I find him locked in corners

staring at the wall
my rage sits bitter on my tongue
my glances piercing arrows from the quiver
I aim at the arrogant doctors who spout medical
lexicon illuminating nothing but the obvious
and the nurses in their bumbling attempts at
promoting his independence
my heart strings have been stretched to capacity
but finally..

stroke (strok) n. a piece of luck; of good for-
tune
i.e. stroke of good luck, stroke of genius

he learns to maneuver his wheelchair
yet his scarred brain, clouded and confused can't
focus too long
on anything
impatient he sails from room to room
can't look at TV, a book or a newspaper
the drone is too rapid for this man of books
doesn't connect in any way
my fledgling must move
his wheelchair, a second leg
I marvel at his speed
some days I actually can't find him - he's flying
up and down hallways, into the elevator
up and down floors - he's flying
to classes
speech therapy, physical therapy
maybe they know what they're doing—

I throw out my expectations...

Reseeding

my morning began with a fast horse
charging through my house
not a fattened, slow pony
drunk on crab apples and sweet straw
but a nervous, shiny-with-sweat
slick, black ghost horse, impatient
woke me with snorts
a fast poem
his foamy steam of winter breath, loaming
kicking at the stall ready to race

I had to approach him slowly, win his trust - I let
him smell
my hands before I touched him
I promised they would give direction
I chose to ride bareback close, my arms around
his neck
my head leaning close to him, skin on skin
our breath mingled
I didn't know what reins to use
then I thought - spruce root, lacing in all my
relations
I would go where he led charging
up Capitol Hill—
is not a mountain
as they butcher this cathedral of pines
you can't clear-cut the Creator
the fabric of spirit glows phosphorescent, foxfire
fossils, outlines of fern, between ghost stalks of
trees
I've seen you stepping
I'm crawling up that hill with you leveling grass
knives in our mouths
I taste the salty brine of rawhide
and the metal of our blood on tongues
counting verbal coup with sharpened pencils
daggers of ink, those ghost trees, songs, chants,
raging raps,

the clan mothers guiding our tongues
as they (knock off the horns) strip them of their
titles
take back these reins of council fires to burn
away this mess

I've seen you naked and worried
about those silver hairs sprouting
in new places threatening to become a lake
when things once hard, now more than not are
soft
brothers with soft edges
sisters becoming hardened
I've seen you in your quaking fear and choking
in your rage so strongly vile   turned inward
causing strokes, high blood pressure, diabetes
and relapses
I've also seen you deep in prayer
in sweats so hot you could barely raise
your head when they raised the flap to air

I've seen you face those
who would "tan your hide" this expression
twisted into words of violence whose origins
 I know something about
as I come from the Pelkeys/Peltiers/pelts - the
"hide skinners"

those tanned skinned ones
my father, my grandmother, those brothers,
cousins and sisters
I give these words for you
in deference to these darker ones I love
they tried locking in dark closets
behind metal doors
calling you the stupid and dangerous
because clear-eyed
you are visionaries
you've become the reseeders
teaching
rapping, speeching and documenting or

silently watching, soberly black-eyed seeing win-
dows
of opportunity as
Bobby, John and Jackie-O went up the hill and
John fell down
'cause they tagged his crown and
Pat and Dick , Ronnie and Nancy and Barbara
and George came tumbling down behind them
Manifest Destiny in reverse because they always
put the cart before this horse
you can't clear-cut the Creator
told us to go back where you came from
smiling as Oklahoma Cherokee make their way
back down the trail to the Mississippi
Eastern Sioux made their way back toward the
hill
the grassy knoll, the burial mound
as we charge up on this sweaty horse
crawl through grass with knives
these brothers and sisters
clear-eyed reseeders in Talking Circles
and Red Road Recovery
and some of us are sleeping with, living with,
loving and married to "the enemy"
and teaching them some songs and chants to
the drum so they breathe and step like us
and some of us carry the enemy within and
on any given day may be mistaken for it

I've seen you and love you all
and some morning he, tanned-skin one, espe-
cially will call her sweetheart
under a star quilt
a bird will call up the morning singing
the smell of cedar and pine over their heads
some morning he will ease her awake
and call her sweetheart
snuggled warm under some star quilt
soft places now becoming hard again
that bird's song calling up the sun

as his hands calling up her thunder
she softens
before one of them bare-assed will freeze in their
dash
to make coffee
for whoever's relative or child
has so gracefully stumbled through the door
while they're busy
reseeding...

Many Tongues Remain

You shot your best shot
played your pattest
hand
and continue to shoot
with Hollywood stereotyping
feathers, arrows
we won't even mention Pocahontas
or those Western wig-wearin' fancydancers
that "original dumb blonde" - Custer
the braid
snakes thick like spruce root
around the wapipi birch bark records

We're not shrunk in your cupboards
we weren't "wiped out"

over 500 nations
our drums sound strong
our dances and languages,
through some dim echoes still intact
many tongues
remain to tell our stories

Don't Mess with Djang Gang

for Rafiq, Aisha, Mohammad, Aziza, Judy, Sandra, Kathy,
Mervyn and all the Powhatan Bostons & Smiths

Don't mess with Djang
she might poke at you
with that
hickory stick
her long
spindly knotted
fingers
jabbing at your
bones
for the truth
you best
"act like you got some sense"

don't mess with Djang
help her trap
the little sparrows
for dinner tonight
she might serve
them up
with mustard greens
or turnip
and that strong
black "medicine"
with it's hints
of chicory

don't mess with Djang
she's whip stitching
on quilts
to cover you with
stars, planets, galaxies
snapping green beans
and shucking
sweet corn
for Kitchie, Bald Eagle and
Newcomer

she don't have time
for no "crumb hustler's" nonsense

don't mess with Djang
she and Mama Liza
are out pickin' wood
betony
to cure your runny nose
and the baby's colic

don't mess with Djang
you best
act like you got some sense

Nokemes
Journey to the Heart

As in a dream
slowly she makes her way
to the water
her moccasined feet
comforted by the
soft carpet of pine needles
loons called to her
from the fog
of her pain

The moon is rising
the water is smooth, still and shiny
obsidian
her silver hair glistens and sparkles
flecks of mica

She greets the moon
Grandmother to Grandmother
raises her pinch of tobacco
to the four directions
proudly for a moment she pauses in the east
as she is Wabanaki, Missisquoi
lingers a moment in the west;
the direction of the loon's call
then releases the offering into the water

She steps lightly
birchbark glides in still waters
holding ash and sweetgrass basket
her mother before her has made
she is dressed in her finest buckskin
beaded with the maple leaf, deer and beaver
with lengths of dried corn and quilled
in the way of her grandmother

She sits erect
facing the moon's glow
in warm, gentle wind brushes her
hair

sings in her ear
she recognizes the whispers of
her people

A smile spreads on her tired
wan face
it crinkles around her eyes
and creates wrinkles
tributaries
linking the waters
to the ocean

She leans back
and surrenders
to her greatest journey
the star bridge
of souls

Heartwashing Song

tears on rock
worn smooth with gentle poundings
Mishomis
blood boiling up
steaming over skin
hairless
blistering, pinked
raising keltoid scars

under a full butter host
Nokemes
heart washing song

washing muscles knotted
and braided
heartwashing song
weary with the impacted bile of
anger, resentments, fears, blames
envies, desires, jealousies
nagging worries
he's sick in prison
she died this morning
he's having seizures
he had a stroke
they got burned out
she got robbed
they got flooded out
they're back in the mix
she's drinking again
he OD'd
she's got cancer
there's been an earthquake
he's been missing
she's got AIDS
he's shot to the curb
she lost her grandmother
the girl's got diabetes
her mother transitted...

short breaths coming in gulps

caffeine driven head poundings
long without
hugs   besitos/"little kisses"
rocking lovemaking
hear the hissing of Grandfather's
breath
breathe deeply the mugwort fisted
tightly
sweetgrass trails
heartwashing song

release
flowing blood unbounded
cleansing liver, kidney
and spleen
flushing with new green shoots
cedar breath
grass sprigs, dandelion roots
hibiscus, soothing with blackberry
mint
sprouted clover

heartwashing song

a lull of voices
quiet pattering
Algonquian, Abenaki, Lakota,
Anishnaabe, Cree
coo of mourning doves
gentle rain on canvas
pour more on those
rocks
salted stream
cedar breath
Shhhhhhhhh!————-

About the Author

Abena Songbird is an Abenaki (French/Irish) poet and singer, a member of the Missisquoi Abenaki of Swanton, Vermont. She was born and lived over 22 Winters in Ndakinna, several years in New Mexico and has spent the last 15 years in the Bay Area.

She was a vocalist in the Glide Ensemble Gospel Choir of Glide Church, San Francisco from 1990 though 1994. In 1998, Abena released her first CD, *They're Calling Us Home.* Composed with her musical collaborator Muhammad Al-Amin, the volume draws on African and indigenous sources to create a contemporary collection of spoken word and jazz In 1996, Abena received the Mary TallMountain Creative Writing and Community Service Award. She is currently the Coordinator for the Native American Cultural Center of San Francisco.

www.ingramcontent.com/pod-product-compliance
Lightning Source LLC
Chambersburg PA
CBHW022031090426
42739CB00006BA/377

* 9 7 8 0 9 1 5 1 1 7 0 6 2 *